D1604795

EMILY OSMENT

Tamra Orr

Mitchell Lane
PUBLISHERS

P.O. Box 196
Hockessin, Delaware 19707
Visit us on the web: www.mitchelllane.com
Comments? email us: mitchelllane@mitchelllane.com

Mitchell Lane
PUBLISHERS

Printing   1   2   3   4   5   6   7   8   9

A Robbie Reader
Contemporary Biography

Abigail Breslin	Albert Pujols	Alex Rodriguez
Aly and AJ	Amanda Bynes	Ashley Tisdale
Brenda Song	Brittany Murphy	Charles Schulz
Dakota Fanning	Dale Earnhardt Jr.	David Archuleta
Demi Lovato	Donovan McNabb	Drake Bell & Josh Peck
Dr. Seuss	Dwayne "The Rock" Johnson	Dylan & Cole Sprouse
Eli Manning	**Emily Osment**	Hilary Duff
Jaden Smith	Jamie Lynn Spears	Jesse McCartney
Jimmie Johnson	Johnny Gruelle	Jonas Brothers
Jordin Sparks	LeBron James	Mia Hamm
Miley Cyrus	Miranda Cosgrove	Raven-Symoné
Selena Gomez	Shaquille O'Neal	Story of Harley-Davidson
Syd Hoff	Tiki Barber	Tom Brady
Tony Hawk		

Library of Congress Cataloging-in-Publication Data
Orr, Tamra.
  Emily Osment / by Tamra Orr.
    p. cm.
  Includes bibliographical references and index.
  ISBN 978-1-58415-755-7 (library bound)
  1. Osment, Emily—Juvenile literature. 2. Television actors and actresses--United States—Juvenile literature. 3. Singers—United States—Biography—Juvenile literature. I. Title.
  PN2287.O725O77 2009
  791.4502'8092—dc22
  [B]

2009012429

ABOUT THE AUTHOR: Tamra Orr is the author of more than 200 books for young people and families, including Mitchell Lane's biographies on Jordin Sparks and Orlando Bloom. A former English teacher, she lives in the Pacific Northwest, where she alternates between her research and looking at the mountains. Orr's books have won several national awards.

PUBLISHER'S NOTE: The following story has been thoroughly researched and to the best of our knowledge represents a true story. While every possible effort has been made to ensure accuracy, the publisher will not assume liability for damages caused by inaccuracies in the data, and makes no warranty on the accuracy of the information contained herein. This story has not been authorized or endorsed by Emily Osment.

TABLE OF CONTENTS

Words in **bold** type can be found in the glossary.

Promoting her shows and movies is one of Emily Osment's favorite parts of her job as an actress. At New York City's Planet Hollywood in April 2009, she celebrated the opening of *Hannah Montana: The Movie.*

That Looks Like Fun

When Emily Jordan Osment was only five years old, she watched as her older brother, Haley Joel, became a superstar almost overnight. As a young boy who "saw dead people" in the M. Night Shyamalan blockbuster movie *The Sixth Sense*, Haley's face and name were suddenly all over the news. Everyone was talking about his amazing performance in the film. Even though he was only eleven years old, he was already being called one of the best child actors of his **generation** (jeh-ner-AY-shun).

Emily was jealous. When she watched her brother working on the set, acting did not seem very difficult. "I thought it looked like so much fun," she told the *[New York] Daily News* in 2007. "I was five at the time. I wanted the attention." She also said that year, "My brother mostly inspired me because I always saw him **rehearsing** [ree-HER-sing] with my dad and going to **auditions** [aw-DIH-shuns]. . . . I asked if I could get into it as well."

She did not have to wait long to find that attention. Around the time she turned six, she was starring in her first commercial. It was an ad for FTD Florists. Emily was hooked—she loved being in the spotlight as much as her brother did. Was it scary? Of course. Was it worth it? Absolutely.

"I was seven and in a TV show **pilot**," Emily said to Naomi Kirsten. "I was about to go onstage for a curtain call, which is when the actors go out and greet the audience. Suddenly I thought, 'Omigosh . . . I can't believe I'm doing this! I can't go out there! There are too many people.' I finally pulled myself together and it ended up being an amazing experience."

A career in front of the camera was definitely part of Emily's future. It was no surprise, either. Her father had been an actor for years. Her brother was being offered

Soon after *The Sixth Sense* came out, the Osment family (Emily, Theresa, Eugene, and Haley Joel) appeared at the International Film Festival. Although the spotlight was on Haley Joel, it would not be long before he began sharing it with his younger sister.

bigger and bigger parts. Now it was time for the youngest member of the family to take her place on the stage—and onscreen.

As the youngest star of the movie *Sarah, Plain and Tall: Winter's End*, Emily grabbed people's attention and was nominated for her first award.

Small Girl, Growing Roles

On March 10, 1992, Emily Osment was born in Los Angeles to Theresa, a skilled seamstress and teacher, and Eugene, an actor. She joined Haley Joel, who had been born in 1988. Once Emily discovered the acting life, even though she was still quite small, her roles began to grow. She did more commercials, including one for McDonald's, plus a radio **spot** with classic television star Dick Van Dyke. She appeared in popular television shows like *Touched by an Angel*, *Friends*, and *3rd Rock from the Sun*. "I watched my dad and brother," she recalled in an interview in 2007. "I guess you could say it runs in the family."

Her fresh face and perky style were noticed quickly. Before 1999 was over, Emily was hired for the role of Miranda Aiken in *The Secret Life of Girls*. She also played Cassie Witting in *Sarah, Plain and Tall: Winter's End*. For the role of Cassie, Emily was **nominated** (NAH-mih-nay-ted) for Best Young Actress Age Ten or Under by the Young Actors Guild. She enjoyed working with costar Christopher Walken. "He's so great around kids," she told Tamara Ikenberg in 2006. "I was little, but I do remember I'd always sit with him and he'd always talk to me."

Next, Emily learned what it was like to act in **animated** (AA-nih-may-ted) movies. She and her brother both acted in *Edwurd Fudwupper Fibbed Big*. In addition, she lent her voice to several Disney film **sequels** (SEE-kwuls), including *The Hunchback of Notre Dame 2*, *Jungle Book 2*, and *Lilo and Stitch 2: Stitch Has a Glitch*. Playing roles like these called for different skills. "You have to use your imagination a lot when you are voicing an animated character," Emily explained in a 2007 interview. "In some ways, it's harder to do

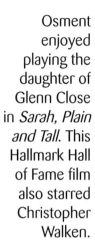

Osment enjoyed playing the daughter of Glenn Close in *Sarah, Plain and Tall*. This Hallmark Hall of Fame film also starred Christopher Walken.

an animated film than it is to do a regular film, because you don't have body language and **facial** [FAY-shyul] expressions at your disposal to really get into the character like you do in regular movies."

Although Emily's acting **résumé** (REH-zuh-may) looked quite amazing for someone so young, her biggest role was still months away. She was about to get the role that would make kids and parents chuckle—and groan—each time she walked onto the scene!

Emily and her brother enjoy going to each other's movie premieres. On July 18, 2002, they attended the first showing of *Spy Kids 2: Island of Lost Dreams.* Both were familiar with being in front of the camera.

Meet Gerti

In 2002, Emily landed the role that would change her career—and get the attention of many young moviegoers across the country: Gerti Giggles. In the beginning, the part in *Spy Kids 2: Island of Lost Dreams* was a small one. But once the **producers** (pruh-DOO-serz) saw Emily act, they began writing more lines and scenes for the character. Gerti Giggles was annoying and adorable enough to get people's attention. "She acts like a grown-up and she knows a lot, but inside her, she's a little girl," Emily wrote on her MySpace page. "She thinks she is the boss of everyone."

In these two movies, Emily was given some amazing stunts. Her most frightening one? "Hanging off a cliff," she wrote. "My stunt

Donning a pair of 3-D glasses, Emily gives the media her famous Gerti Giggles smile at the premiere of *Spy Kids 3-D* in 2003.

girl was even younger than I am. There were sharp rocks and I was in a harness. I've rock climbed before and been in a harness, plus the crew teaches you how to stay safe. That scene took . . . half a day." Gerti Giggles was popular enough that she and Emily were brought back for the 2003 sequel, *Spy Kids 3-D: Game Over.*

When Emily was hired to play the part of Cassie Keller in *The Haunting Hour: Don't Think About It,* she had to laugh. The movie was based on a story by young adult horror author R. L. Stine—and she had never been

On the set of *The Haunting Hour*, Emily got the chance to completely change her looks and her attitude. In this movie, she was sinister and dark—nothing like her role as Gerti Giggles.

brave enough to read any of his books. Yet here she was in one of his movies. As Cassie, she was able to behave in ways that were nothing like her. "I got to be mean and nasty to my [onscreen] parents and be **Goth**," she said in an *Emily Osment World* interview. "It was a completely different experience, and it felt really good to play her."

Playing other people came naturally to Emily—which was a good thing. There were quite a few roles waiting for her just around the corner.

These two friends are often seen together: Emily and superstar Miley Cyrus. Whether in front of the camera or appearing at a celebrity event, the two girls enjoy each other's company.

Hannah's New Best Friend

After starring in her first scary movie, Emily tackled a number of other roles. In 2008, she played Becca in *Soccer Mom*, acting along with her dad, who played the character of Marty. She was also cast in another animated movie, *Surviving Sid*. The following year, she was given the role of Melissa Hamilton in the TV movie *Dadnapped*.

As many fans as Emily already had, it was nothing compared to the number she created after she won the next role for which she auditioned. She was called in to try out for the part of Lilly Truscott, the best friend of Hannah Montana, played by teen superstar Miley

Cyrus. *Hannah Montana* became one of Disney Channel's hottest shows.

Osment auditioned four times before she won the role of Lilly and her alter ego, Lola Luftnagle. She got the role—and a new teenage star joined the Disney Channel lineup. She loves the part, although she and Lilly are not a lot alike. "Lilly is a huge drama queen and I'm pretty relaxed," she told Naomi Kirsten in 2007. "Lilly is sporty and I love soccer, snowboarding, and golf, so that's where we connect."

That's the way she likes it, however. "Actors pull from their own experiences to bring reality [ree-AL-ih-tee] to the characters," she adds. "I wouldn't want to play someone who's a lot like me. There would be no turning it on or off."

As more and more young people have come to recognize Emily, it has gotten harder for her to go out in public. "You can't really go out a lot," she admitted to Richard Huff of the *[New York] Daily News.* "When I go out with my family and friends, it's tough. No matter how much you cover up, they know it's you."

Having fun with friends Miley Cyrus and Lucas Till is part of being on one of Disney's hottest shows. At the screening for *Hannah Montana: The Movie*, the three costars enjoyed clowning around for the camera.

At Camp McDonald's 16th annual family Halloween carnival, Emily—and her scarecrow friend—helped raise money for charity.

Since many of Emily's fans are young girls, she knows that she is also a role model. "You have this incredible fan base of kids that are seven and eight," she told Huff. "These kids get to look up to us, which is a great feeling."

Emily has been involved in a number of **charity** (CHAYR-ih-tee) events. She took part in the 10th Annual L.A. Cancer Challenge and appeared at a conference with St. Jude Research Hospital. There she worked to raise money to help critically ill children. At the 2007 Disney Channel Games, she played to support the UNICEF Foundation. She joined CosmoGIRL for an online charity auction. In 2008, she was also part of Disney's Earth Day event, teaching kids about the importance of helping the environment.

Emily stops to smile for her fans before she walks into the Jonas Brothers' 3-D concert. Like so many other young people, Emily is a huge fan of this popular group.

Into the Future

What does the future hold for Emily Osment? Before she turned eighteen, she was exploring going into music. She performed the theme song for *The Haunting Hour* and enjoyed every minute of it. She was in her school choir, plus she has a singing coach. Could music one day take over for acting?

"When it comes to singing and acting, I don't think I could choose," she said in an *Emily Osment World* interview. "I have been acting for a much longer time, but singing is something I love to do. It was a hobby that turned into a job. I definitely want to pursue it more. But right now, I am focused on acting."

While Osment's face can be found in multiple magazines—and it's on television almost all the time—she insists that she is still just a regular teen. She credits her parents with that. "It all goes back to family. My parents have done a great job **managing** [MAA-nuh-jing] us through school and work," she admitted in the same interview.

Emily's father agrees. In a 2007 *New York Times* interview, he said, "We do our best to be an average American family. When we come home from work, we do everything from doing the dishes after dinner to cleaning up dog poop in the yard."

Until 2007, Emily stayed in public school, but then she turned to **independent** (in-dee-PEN-dunt) study. "It is hard to balance acting with my normal life," she told Naomi Kirsten, "but I have great friends and family who keep me balanced with my independent study classes and just being a normal kid."

Osment has helpful advice for other young girls like herself. "Fear is the biggest thing keeping you from living your dreams,"

Emily credits her mother for helping her develop her own style of music. "I play the guitar and so does my brother and my mom," she says. "We've always gone around singing."

At the 2008 Creative Arts Emmy Awards in September, Emily could look forward to a full and exciting future. It is easy to understand why she says, "I wanna do this [acting] till I die!"

she said. "You should really branch out and try something new—something you never thought you'd be good at. If you try something new, it will lead to other things, and eventually you'll find something you're *really* passionate about. And *that's* what it's all about!"

CHRONOLOGY

1992 Emily Jordan Osment is born in Los Angeles on March 10.

1998 She makes her acting debut in a commercial for FTD Florists.

1999 Emily appears in her first movie, *The Secret Life of Girls*.

2000 She lends her voice to the animated film *Edwurd Fudwupper Fibbed Big*.

2002 She is cast as Gerti Giggles in the *Spy Kids* movies.

2006 She joins the cast of Disney Channel's *Hannah Montana*.

2007 She records her first official song for the movie *The Haunting Hour: Don't Think About It*. She leaves school to have private instruction on the set of *Hannah Montana*.

2009 She plays Lilly Truscott in *Hannah Montana: The Movie*.

FILMOGRAPHY

2009 *Dadnapped*

Hannah Montana: The Movie

2008 *Soccer Mom*

Surviving Sid

2007 *The Haunting Hour: Don't Think About It*

2006 *Hannah Montana* (TV series)

Holidaze: The Christmas That Almost Didn't Happen

2005 *Lilo and Stitch 2: Stitch Has a Glitch*

2003 *Spy Kids 3-D: Game Over*

2002 *Spy Kids 2: Island of Lost Dreams*

2001 *Friends* (TV series; guest appearance)

2000 *Edwurd Fudwupper Fibbed Big*

Touched by an Angel (TV series; guest appearance)

1999 *The Secret Life of Girls*

Sarah, Plain and Tall: Winter's End

3rd Rock from the Sun (TV series; guest appearance)

FIND OUT MORE

Books

If you enjoyed this book about Emily Osment, you might also enjoy the following Robbie Reader Contemporary Biographies from Mitchell Lane Publishers:

Ashley Tisdale
Brenda Song
Demi Lovato
Dylan and Cole Sprouse
The Jonas Brothers
Miley Cyrus
Miranda Cosgrove
Raven-Symoné
Selena Gomez

Works Consulted

Blair, E. "Emily Osment Tells All". September 7, 2007. Emily Osment World
    http://www.emilyosment.us/interviews/emily2007.php?subaction=sh
    owfull&id=1189970005&archive=&start_from=&ucat=17&

Boursaw, Jane Louise. "Emily Osment of R.L. Stine's *The Haunting Hour*."
    Blend Television, September 14, 2007.
    http://www.cinemablend.com/television/INTERVIEW-Emily-Osment-
    of-R-L-Stine-s-The-Haunting-Hour-6354.html

Emily Osment: MySpace.
    http://profile.myspace.com/
    index.cfm?fuseaction=user.viewprofile&friendid=222764292; and
    http://profile.myspace.com/
    index.cfm?fuseaction=user.viewProfile&friendID=198843300

Huff, Richard. " 'Hannah Montana' Is Manna to Emily Osment." *[New York]
    Daily News*. December 6, 2007.
    http://www.nydailynews.com/entertainment/tv/2007/12/06/
    2007-12-06_hannah_montana_is_manna_to_emily_osment.html

FIND OUT MORE

Ikenberg, Tamara. "Osment Makes Her Own Fame." *The [Louisville, KY] Courier-Journal*, June 24, 2006.
http://www.emilyosment.us/interviews/
2006interviews.php?subaction=showfull&id=1187129187&archive=&
start_from=&ucat=19&

Kaikowski, Geri Anne. "Emily Osment Makes Stop at Steamtown Mall Sunday." *Emily Osment World, n.d.*;
http://www.emilyosment.us/interviews/emily2007

Kirsten, Naomi. "Emily Osment." *Emily Osment World, n.d.*.
http://www.emilyosment.us/interviews/emity2007

Navarro, Mireya. "When Childhood Is a Tough Role." *The New York Times.* September 23, 2007.
http://query.nytimes.com/gst/
fullpage.html?res=9D06E0D91339F930A1575AC0A9619C8B63

On the Internet

Emily Osment World
http://www.emilyosment.us/

Emily Osment TV.com
http://www.tv.com/emily-osment/person/41278/summary.html

Emily Osment at Kidzworld
http://www.kidzworld.com/article/7212-emily-osment-biography

GLOSSARY

animated (AA-nih-may-ted)—A style or type of film that is made up of drawn characters which move and talk.

audition (aw-DIH-shun)—To try out for a part in a play, movie, or other type of performance.

charity (CHAYR-ih-tee)—An organization that uses money and donations to help people in need.

facial (FAY-shyul)—Of or for the face.

generation (jeh-ner-AY-shun)—A group of people born and living at about the same time.

Goth (GAHTH)—A style of dressing and acting that usually involves wearing black clothing and heavy makeup.

independent (in-dee-PEN-dunt)—Not controlled by others; not relying on others for aid or support.

managing (MAA-nuh-jing)—Taking care or charge of.

nominated (NAH-mih-nay-ted)—To propose someone to win a contest, prize or award.

pilot (PY-lit)—The first episode of a show taped in order to convince a network to adopt the show as a series.

producer (pruh-DOO-ser)—The person who creates or is responsible for the production of a television show or film.

rehearsing (ree-HER-sing)—Practicing lines and movements for a future performance.

résumé (REH-zuh-may)—An official list of jobs or other activities a person has accomplished.

sequel (SEE-kwul)—A follow-up to a story, often in books and film.

spot (in radio)—A commercial or short announcement.

INDEX